MINDBENDERS

INTRODUCTION

This book is called *Mindbenders*, but the original title was *The Shapes of Mathematics*. It was changed because the editors thought that the 'mathematics' part sounded a bit dull, and maybe they were right. For example, if I asked *you* to give a definition of 'mathematics', what would you say? The chances are you'd talk about numbers and the four rules of addition, subtraction, multiplication and division, or you might be braver and talk about shapes and graphs. But unless you're really adventurous, you probably wouldn't make links between maths and paintings, sea shells and railway lines.

Well, when you've worked through this book, I hope you'll make those links, and many others, and come to realise that there's more to mathematics than crunching numbers.

Mindbenders combines information with activities. Some of the activities need time and effort – but there's no need to do all of the experiments in one go, so keep coming back until you've tried them all. Get ready for a tour of mathematical ideas that spans two thousand years of history – and enjoy the trip!

Written by John Eden
Illustrated by Archie Plumb

Collins Educational
An imprint of HarperCollinsPublishers

CHAPTER 1 – CURVES, POLYOMINOES AND DISSECTIONS

CURVES

The Sand Pendulum

In the 1960s, a toy appeared which was used to draw patterns based on curved lines. Similar patterns can be made using:

- string
- an empty washing-up liquid bottle
- a bag of sand

1 Thoroughly wash out and dry the washing-up liquid bottle, and carefully make a small hole in the bottom (making sure it is big enough to take the string).

2 Make a big knot in the string, and thread it through the bottle from the inside. This is tricky – you may need to hook it through with a piece of wire:

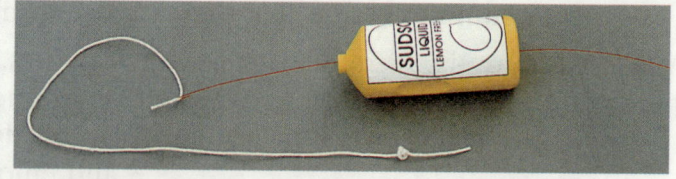

3 Pull the string so that the knot is firm against the base of the bottle, then cut it so that about 40cm sticks out:

CURVES, POLYOMINOES AND DISSECTIONS

4 Tie the string and bottle to the middle of another piece of string about 2m long. Tie the long string so that the bottle hangs just above the floor. Use firm supports:

5 Check that the bottle swings freely, and then fill it with sand. Place a big piece of paper underneath, and set the bottle swinging. The pouring sand should make an attractive pattern on the paper:

To keep a permanent copy of the pattern, paint the paper with PVA glue before starting, so that the sand will stick.

If there are any problems, try using different lengths of string.

These patterns are called **Lissajou figures**, after the French mathematician, Jules Lissajou, who first described curves like this. The mathematical description of Lissajou figures can be very complicated, but essentially they are produced by combining two movements travelling in different directions.

3

Curves from Straight Lines

The Lissajou figure produced with the sand pendulum will generally be made of curved lines. It is possible, however, to make curves by using straight lines. These are called **envelope curves**.

This is a simple example that can form the basis for patterns as complicated as you wish to make them.

1 Draw two lines at an angle and mark an equal number of points on each, numbering as shown:

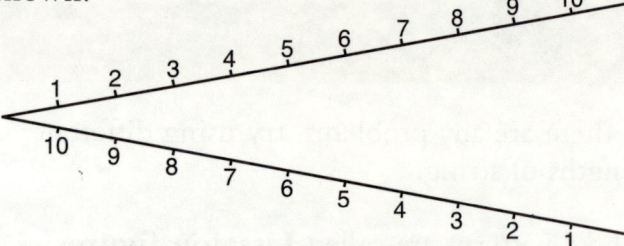

2 Now join 1 to 1, 2 to 2, 3 to 3 and so on:

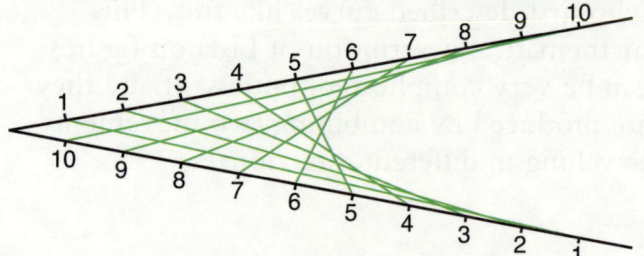

A curve should result.

A range of patterns and pictures can be produced using this basic envelope curve method.

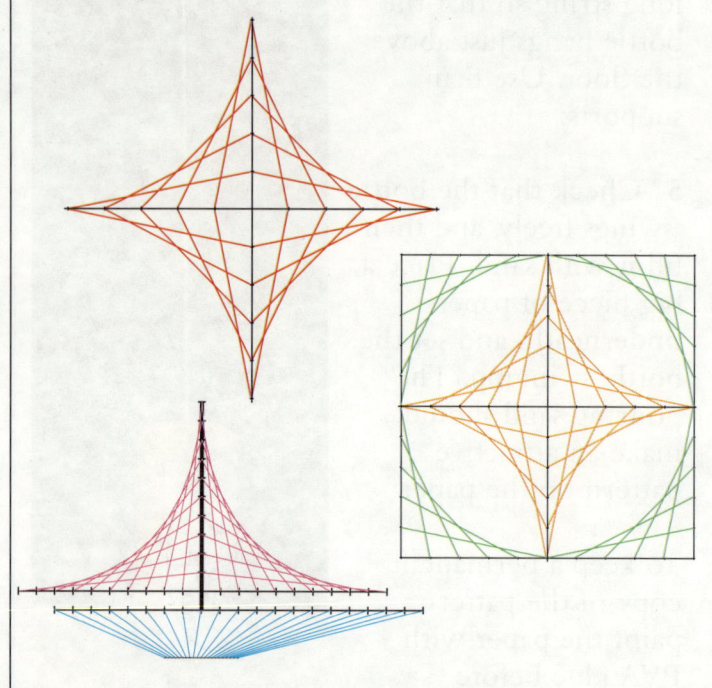

The curves above are produced from numbered straight-line frames, but it's also possible to use curved frames.

CURVES, POLYOMINOES AND DISSECTIONS

1 Draw round a circular protractor.

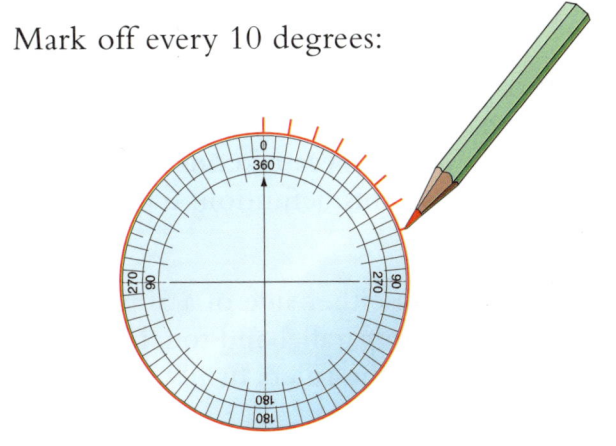

2 Mark off every 10 degrees:

3 Number the points 1 to 36:

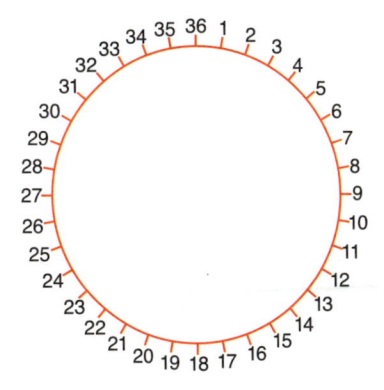

4 Go round the circle again, this time numbering only even numbers up to 70:

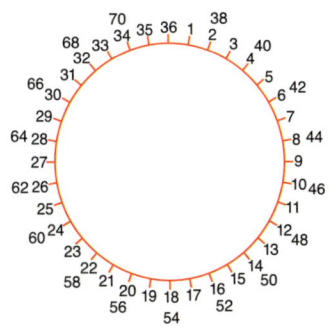

5 Starting at 1, go round the circle and, with a ruler, join each number to its double. That is, join 1 to 2, 2 to 4, 3 to 6, 4 to 8, 5 to 10 and so on until the last line, which joins 35 to 70:

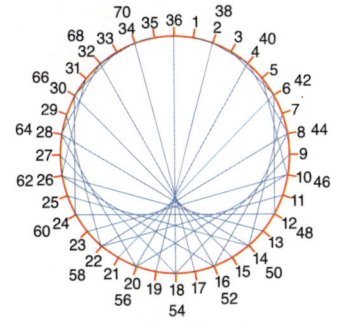

This will produce a curve called a **cardioid**, so-called because of its heart-shaped appearance.

5

CURVES, POLYOMINOES AND DISSECTIONS

Envelope curves can be drawn in pen or pencil, fine felt pen or sharp coloured pencil. But another very attractive effect results from stitching them onto fairly thick card.

1 Draw the frames on the card and, after marking the points, pierce them through with a needle.

2 Now, instead of drawing straight lines, stitch them with coloured cotton, or embroidery silk. The thread need not be too long. When it runs out, simply sticky tape the end of the thread to the back of the card and start with more thread:

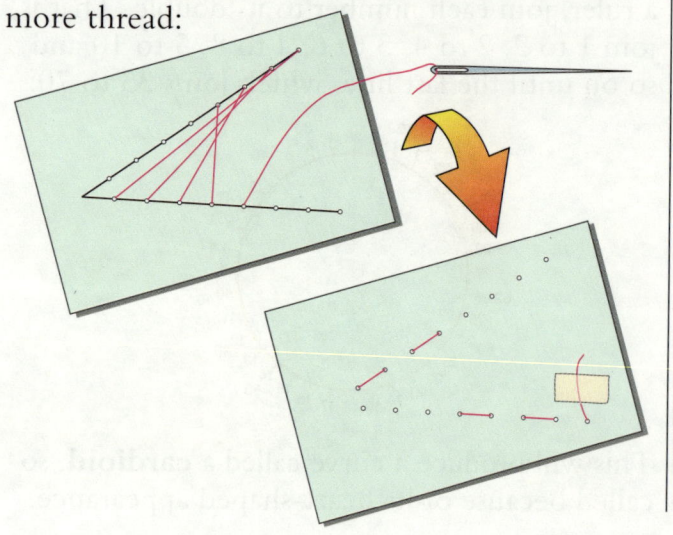

Curves of Constant Width

The differences between 20p and 50p coins and other denominations are very obvious – the twenty and the fifty both have seven sides.

What isn't so obvious is that, mathematically speaking, they are **curves of constant width**.

To understand this definition, try this experiment:

1 Put a ruler on either side of a 50p piece so that the rulers are parallel and touching the coin. Sticky tape the rulers firmly in place:

The coin can be rotated to any position, but will still touch both rulers.

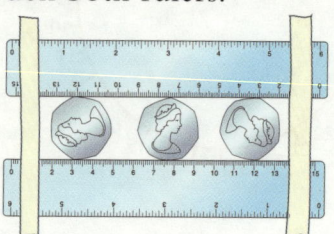

6

This is because it is a curve of constant width, and no matter where you measure across the full width of the coin, the result is always the same. The 20p piece has the same property. Both coins are **constant width curve heptagons**.

Drawing a 50p piece

Draw a circle of radius 5cm and divide it into **sectors** with angles of 51.5 degrees. (Actually the angles should be 360 ÷ 7, which is 51.43, but your protractor won't give you that accuracy.

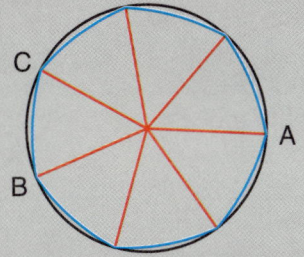

Now, with the point of the compasses at A, draw an arc between B and C. Continue this around the circle until all seven curved sides are complete.

The information panel shows how to draw the heptagon curve, but it is possible to draw an easier **constant width curve** by following these instructions:

1 Set a pair of compasses to any radius (around 8cm will work well), and draw a long arc on card.

2 Then put the point of the compasses on the arc, near the end, (marked Y on the diagram) and draw another arc to cross the first.

3 Finally, put the point of the compasses at X, and draw a third arc to cross the first two. The result, in this case, is a constant width curve triangle.

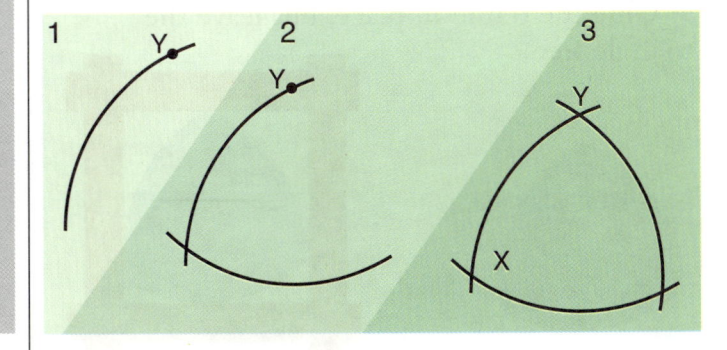

7

CURVES, POLYOMINOES AND DISSECTIONS

To understand an important property of the constant width curve triangle, try the following:

1 Cut out the constant width triangle and also four straight strips of card.

2 Use the strips of card to make a square frame that fits around and touches the triangle:

3 Glue the frame in place, but leave the triangle free:

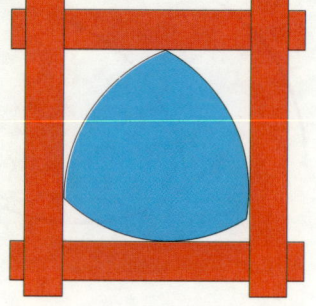

The result is that the triangle can be freely rotated within the frame, but will touch all the sides of the square at all times.

This property of the constant width triangle is behind the principle of the **Wankel engine** and the **Watts drill**.

The Engine and the Drill

The constant width curve triangle shape is used in the Wankel engine (pronounced Vankel) found in some cars and motorcycles, in which a spinning rotor is used rather than the more conventional pistons.

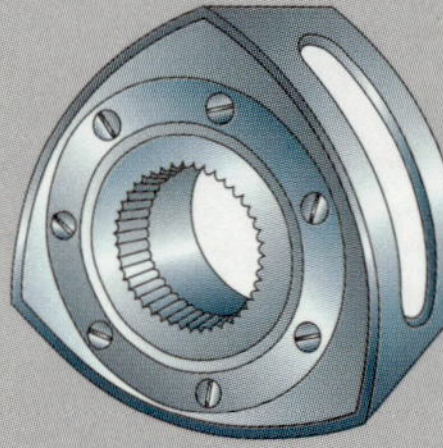

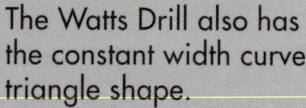

The Watts Drill also has the constant width curve triangle shape.

Used in a special 'chuck', this drill will produce square holes!

8

CURVES, POLYOMINOES AND DISSECTIONS

A Curious Roller – more about the constant width curve triangle.

For thousands of years, the roller has been used to shift heavy loads. For example, it is thought that the giant stones of Stonehenge were moved on rollers.

Rollers are always cylindrical – that is, if you look at the end, you see a circle. It is possible, however, to make a non-cylindrical roller using the constant width curve triangle:

1 Draw round the triangle onto stiff card to make four curves, and mount them on axles. (The axles might be a piece of wood or a roll of card, but make sure the material is stiff and firmly attached to the centre of each curve):

2 Now put a piece of board on top of the rollers and push it along:

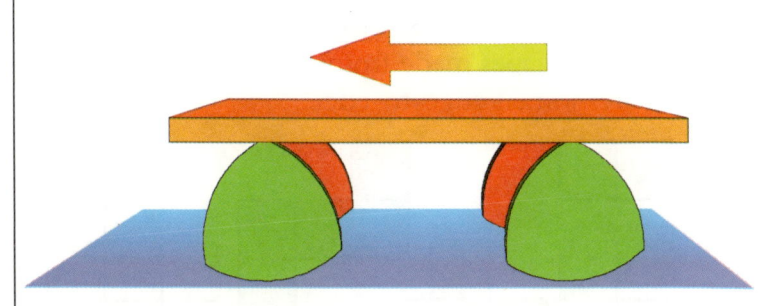

The effect is very odd. Seen from the side, the rollers will appear to be making a lumpy progress, but the board itself will ride along smoothly.

So, surprisingly, a constant width curve triangle can be used as a roller, but what happens if it is used as a wheel? Try making a simple wheelbarrow with an axle through the centre of the curve.

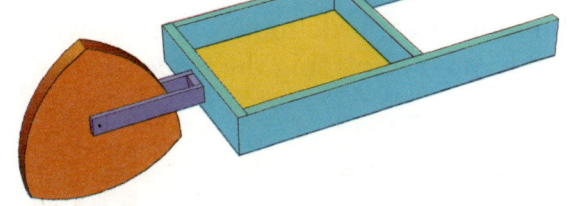

POLYOMINOES

In 1953, an American mathematician, Solomon Golomb, invented the name **polyominoes** to describe shapes made from various numbers of squares joined edge-to-edge.

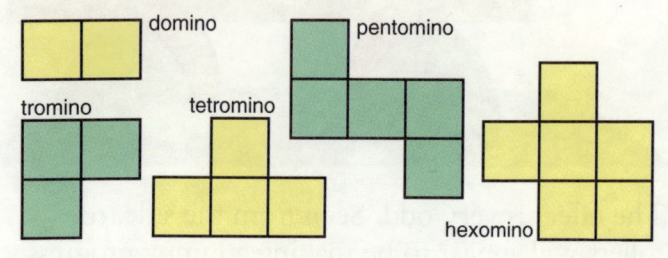

There is only one domino, because although it might be moved around, the two squares always make the same shape.

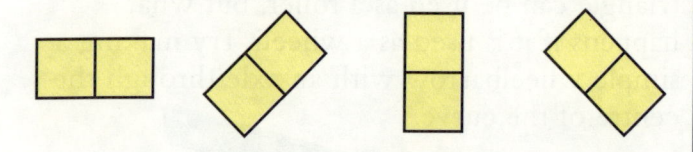

Trominoes are a little more exciting, with two possible ways of placing the three squares.

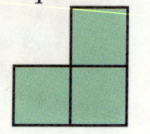

However, from then onwards, things become more interesting. There are:

  5 tetrominoes (arrangements of four squares)
  12 pentominoes (arrangements of five squares)
  35 hexominoes (arrangements of six squares)

Try to draw the full arrangements for each of the polyomino groups above. (See answers, pages 46–47.)

Tiling patterns

Polyomino sets can be used to make tiling patterns (or **tessellations**) like those below.

Each shape tessellates with itself.

One of each of the 12 pentominoes (five square **nets**) will fit together inside a rectangle of six by ten squares. There is more than one way to make them fit together, and, in fact, it has been calculated that there are 2339 ways to make the rectangle. Finding even one way is fairly difficult, but try to complete the one below.

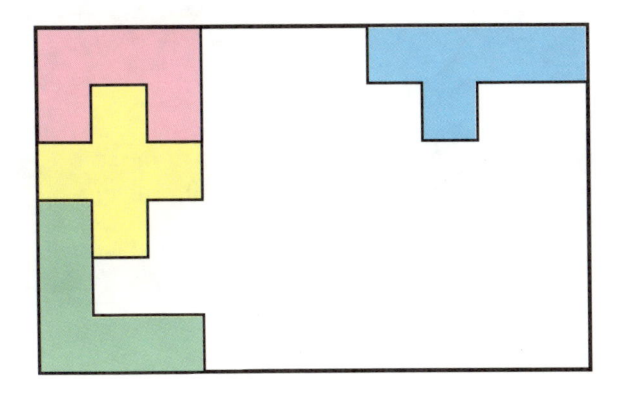

It might be easier to complete the rectangle by cutting the pentominoes from card and using them like jigsaw puzzle pieces. (See answers, pages 46-47.)

Cubes and boxes

The nets of some hexominoes will fold up into cubes if they are cut out. For example:

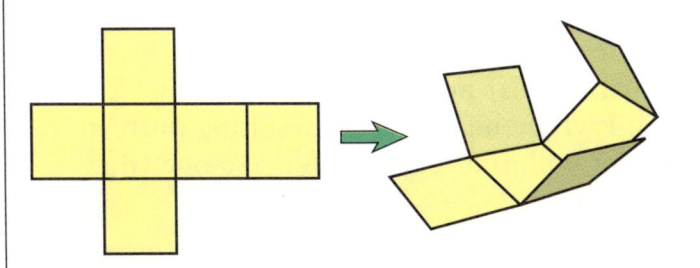

This one may not be so obvious, but it does work.

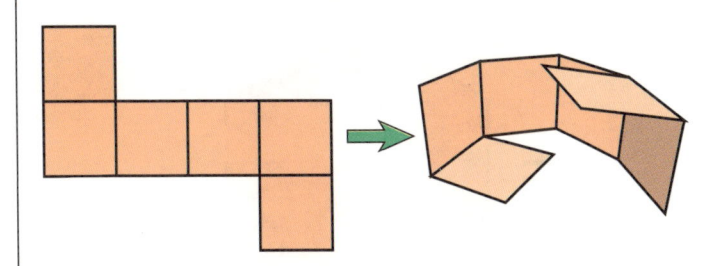

There are 11 hexominoes (six square nets) that can be used to make a cube. See how many you can find. (See answers, pages 46-47.)

11

CURVES, POLYOMINOES AND DISSECTIONS

DISSECTIONS

Mathematicians use the technique of dissection to find out the properties of geometrical shapes.

For example, if you dissect, or cut up, two equal, regular hexagons as shown and add a third whole hexagon, the resulting thirteen pieces will join together to make one large hexagon.

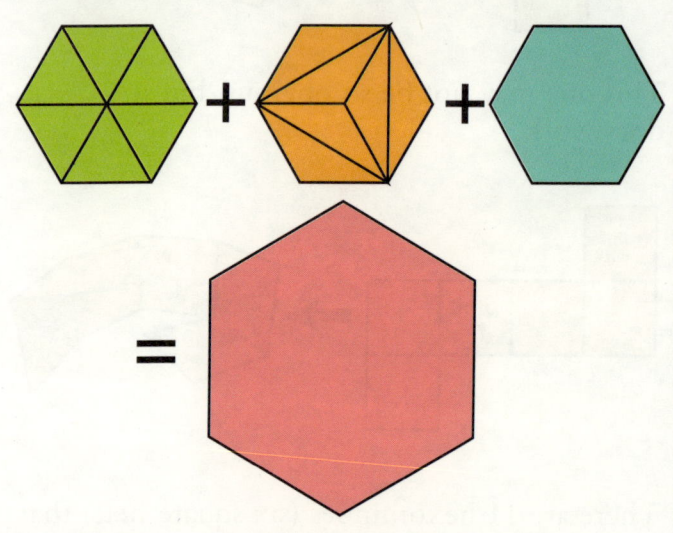

See if you can complete it. (See answers, pages 46-47.)

How to Draw a Regular Hexagon

Draw a circle with a pair of compasses and then, keeping the radius the same, 'step off' arcs around the circumference of the circle. Each time, the new position of the point of the compasses is the previous arc.

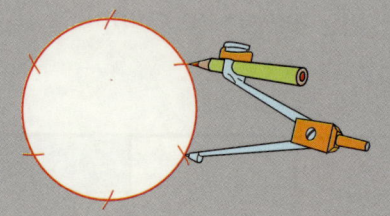

When complete, join the six arcs to make a regular hexagon – that is, one with all sides and angles the same.

Tangrams

Mathematical dissections come from a very ancient tradition. **Tangrams** is a Chinese game for which there are written records dating back to 2000BC. The seven tangram pieces are made from a square.

CURVES, POLYOMINOES AND DISSECTIONS

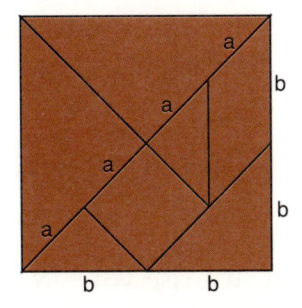

Use the diagram above to make your own tangram shapes.

1 Draw a square on card. (The lines marked 'a' are the same length as one another and the lines marked 'b' are the same length as one another).

2 Then mark and cut out the pieces.

Napoleon Bonaparte enjoyed playing tangrams so he can be used as the example of how the game is played. Arrange your pieces so that, with a little imagination, his outline can be seen.

Now try the puzzles below. In each case, use all seven pieces to create the shape that is shown in silhouette.

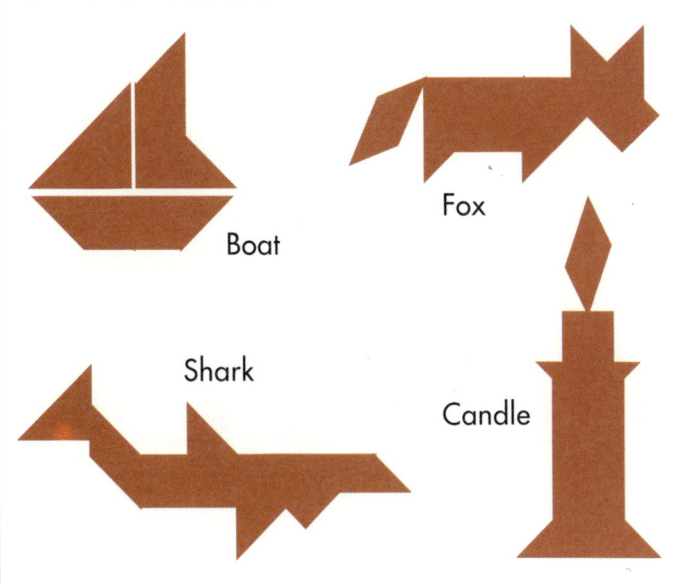

Boat

Fox

Shark

Candle

Now try to make:
   a rectangle
   a triangle
   a parallelogram (See answers, pages 46–47.)

Try to invent your own tangrams, but remember, the rules of tangrams say that all seven pieces must be used each time.

13

CURVES, POLYOMINOES AND DISSECTIONS

Vanishing Squares
The technique of dissection can also make squares disappear. To demonstrate this, try the following:

1 Draw the square below onto 1cm squared paper:

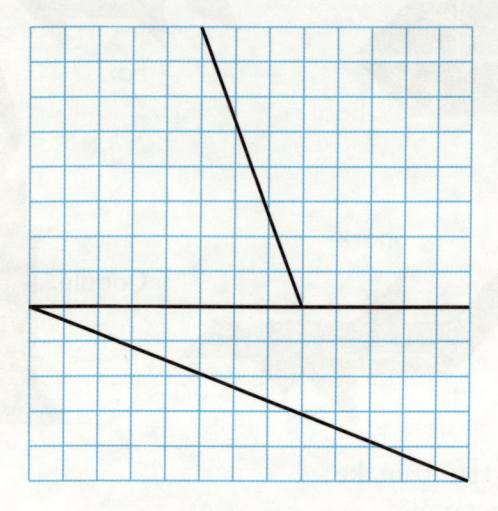

2 Add the dark lines, keeping all measurements accurate.

3 Write down the area of the square.

4 Now dissect the square into four pieces by cutting along the dark lines, and rearrange the pieces into a single rectangle.

5 Now find the area of the rectangle.

Does the result surprise you? (See answers, pages 46–47.)

14

CHAPTER 2 – MATHS IN ART AND MATHS IN NATURE

MATHS IN ART

M C Escher, and more Tessellations

Look at these pictures of pieces of wood nailed together. It might look quite possible to make these shapes, but, in fact, they can only exist as two-dimensional drawings.

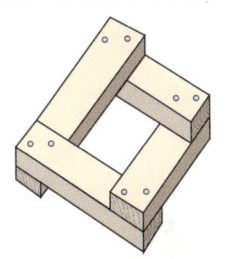

The Dutch artist, Maurits Escher (1898 – 1972), is famous for his lithographs of impossible scenes. Here is an example:

Cordon Art BV

Escher also produced many works based on tessellations. He was inspired by visits to the Alhambra in Granada, Spain, where the tile patterns fascinated him. Escher went on to produce patterns like this:

Cordon Art BV

He wrote, 'This is the richest source of inspiration I have ever struck. A surface can be regularly filled up with similar-shaped figures without leaving any open spaces.'

15

MATHS IN ART AND MATHS IN NATURE

To produce tile patterns like Escher's:

1 Take a square piece of card about 6cm by 6cm.

2 Cut an odd shape from the right-hand edge:

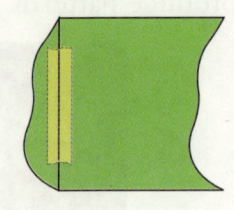

3 Sticky tape the shape to the left-hand edge.

4 Do the same thing with the top edge, sticky taping the shape to the bottom edge:

This makes a tile that will tessellate. The one shown above makes this pattern.

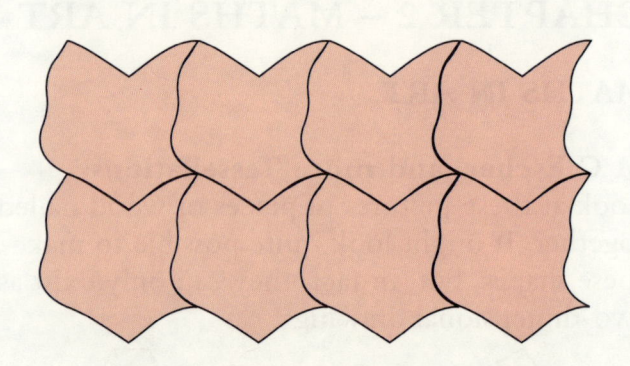

As you look at it, can you see somebody with wavy hair and a long nose?

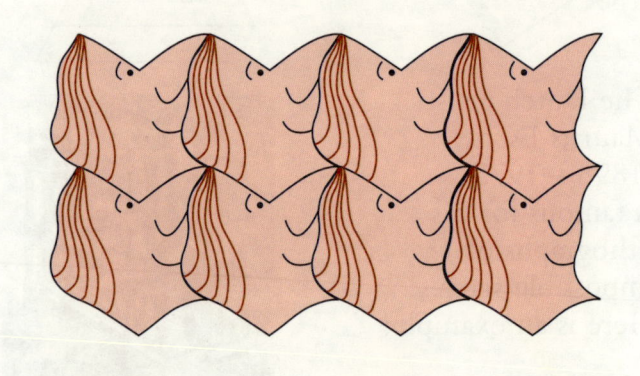

Now try this with your own tiles.

Fibonacci Numbers

Leonardo of Pisa (1170 – 1250) was the greatest mathematician of the Middle Ages. He made a number of important contributions to mathematics, one of which was the **Fibonacci numbers**. This is the famous Fibonacci series that Leonardo described.

1, 1, 2, 3, 5, 8, 13, 21, __, __, __, __, __, __,

Try to work out how the series is produced and continue it until there are twenty numbers in the series. The twentieth number should be 6765. (See answers, pages 46-47.)

A LATIN LESSON
Leonardo was the son of Bonaccus. In Latin this would be written as 'filius Bonacci' – or, for short, 'Fibonacci'.

Now use the Fibonacci series to try these calculations. (A calculator will be helpful.)

1 Take any three consecutive numbers (e.g., 8, 13, 21) and multiply the middle one by itself (e.g., 13 x 13).

2 Then multiply the other two together (e.g., 8 x 21).

3 Note the result.

Try this again with several groups of numbers from the series. Is there a pattern in the result? (See answers, pages 46-47.)

Now use a calculator and divide each number by the number in front of it in the series (e.g., 1÷1, 2÷1, 3÷2, 5÷3, and so on). Write down the answers and see if there is anything surprising in the results. (See answers, pages 46-47.)

MATHS IN ART AND MATHS IN NATURE

The Golden Section
Look at this rectangle. Measure its length (L) and width (W) in millimetres and then calculate L ÷ W.

Does the answer look familiar?

This rectangle is called a **golden rectangle**. Any rectangle with length and width in the ratio 1.6 to 1 – the golden ratio – is called a golden rectangle. For example, these rectangles are all different sizes, but they're all golden. L ÷ W is 1.6 in each case.

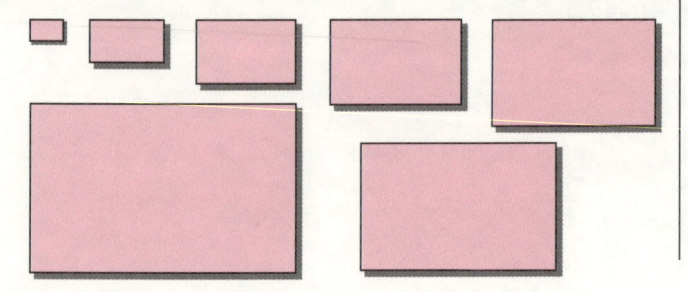

Golden rectangles are considered to have ideal proportions. For thousands of years the golden ratio of 1.6 to 1 has appeared in art and architecture. Strictly, the exact ratio is 1.618 to 1, but 1.6 to 1 is used for convenience. For example, the Parthenon at Athens fits almost exactly into a golden rectangle.

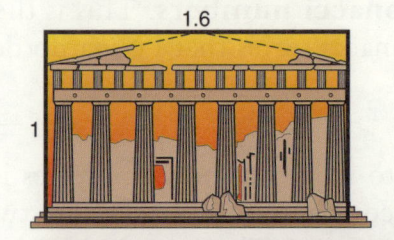

And in this painting *Saint Jerome* by Leonardo da Vinci (1452 – 1519), the main figure of the saint can be enclosed in a golden rectangle.

Vatican Museums and Galleries, Rome/Bridgeman Art Library, London

18

Draw a Golden Rectangle

Start with a square and measure the mid-point of the bottom edge.

Then draw an arc as shown to meet the extended bottom edge:

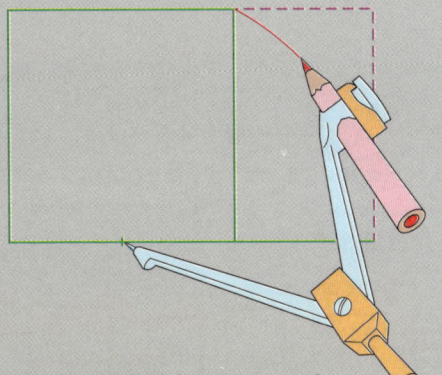

Complete your golden rectangle as shown. Check that L ÷ W comes to about 1.6 to be sure it is golden.

Another method is:

Draw the Width, then multiply that number by 1.6 to get the Length; or draw the Length, then divide that number by 1.6 to get the Width.

A Nest of Golden Rectangles

Draw a golden rectangle on tracing paper or on a sheet of clear acetate, and then draw in a diagonal:

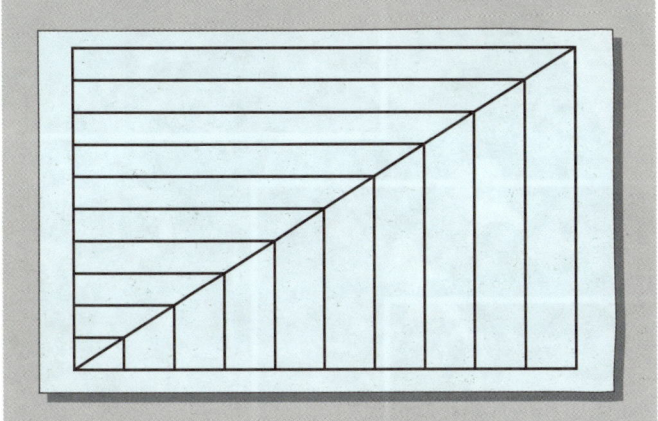

Now add more rectangles. By proportion, they'll all be golden. (You could check by calculating L ÷ W).

The German artist, Albrecht Durer (1471 - 1528), painted this picture, *The Adoration of the Magi*.

Look at the gifts being presented to Jesus. Lines have been added to place the gifts at the corners of rectangles. For each rectangle, measure length and width in millimetres and calculate L ÷ W.

Da Vinci and Durer were by no means alone in using golden rectangles in their art. If you look at the abstract paintings of Piet Mondrian (1872 - 1945) you'll find many golden rectangles, and it was said of the neo-impressionist, Georges Seurat (1859 - 1891), that 'He attacks every canvas with the golden ratio'.

A Rectangle Survey

Draw a selection of rectangles on a sheet of paper and number them. Make one of them a golden rectangle.

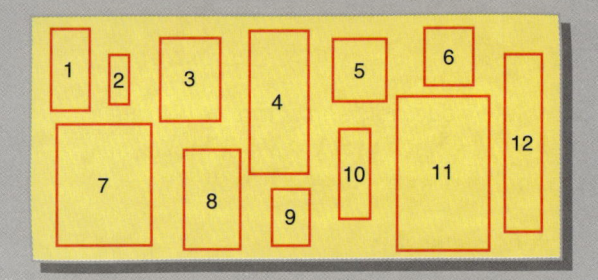

Now ask people to vote for the rectangle whose shape they find most pleasing. Does the golden rectangle win?

Find some examples of paintings by Seurat and look for groups of figures in them. Use your golden rectangle nest to see if they fit the golden ratio. Try this with paintings by Mondrian too, and works by other artists – it may be surprising how often golden rectangles enclose important details and groups.

MATHS IN NATURE

Mathematical bodies

A French architect and painter, Le Corbusier (1887 – 1965), believed in this golden proportion. He worked out a system of ideal proportions that he called 'Le Modulor'. Le Corbusier based it on the averages he calculated from measurements made on thousands of adults, and suggested that it should be the basis for the dimensions of houses and furniture. The following diagram is based on his sketches for the average dimensions of the adult male.

platform heights
in centimetres

27   43   70   86   113   140   183   226

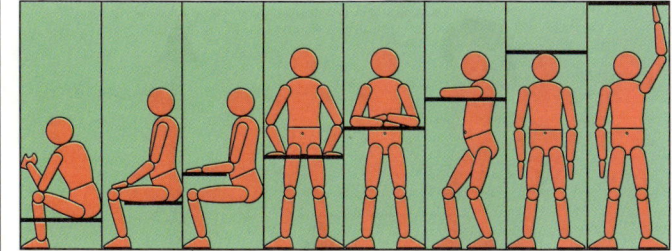

These platform heights could be used in designing work surfaces and various pieces of furniture.

Try playing with Le Corbusier's platform height numbers. Are there two Fibonacci-type sequences? Can you produce the golden ratio by dividing pairs of numbers? (See answers, pages 46-47.)

MATHS IN ART AND MATHS IN NATURE

This experiment has links with le Corbusier:

1 Measure your height, standing without shoes on.

2 Then measure the height of your navel above the floor:

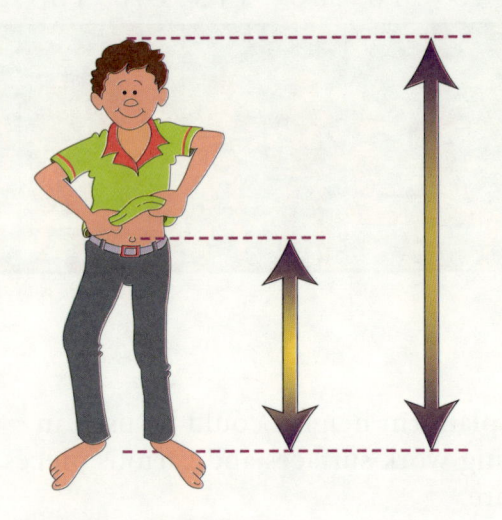

3 Now calculate height ÷ navel height and note the result.

Try this with lots of people and compare results. (See answers, pages 46–47.)

Spirals and Shells

The golden ratio in nature can be explored in another way, by drawing a golden rectangle (see page 19) on an A4 sheet of paper.

1 When the golden rectangle has been drawn, mark off a square.

2 Calculate L ÷ W for this rectangle. Is the rectangle golden?

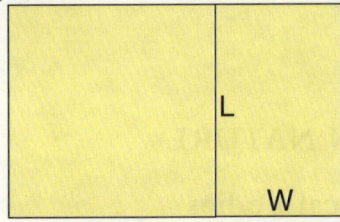

3 Now divide off a square in the small rectangle, and in the next small rectangle, and the next, and so on until the diagram is too small to work on:

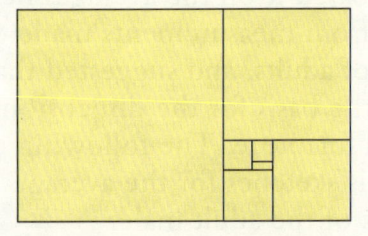

22

MATHS IN ART AND MATHS IN NATURE

4 Then use a pair of compasses to draw arcs with centres at 1, 2, 3, 4 and so on:

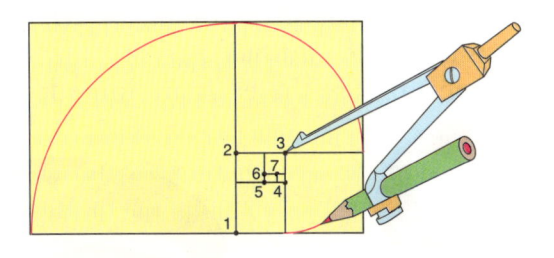

The result should be a spiral.

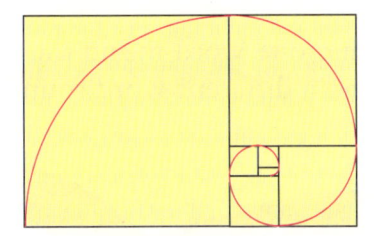

In mathematics, spirals like this, drawn in the golden rectangle, are called equiangular, because the curve of the spiral makes the same angle with any radius drawn from its centre.

In the previous illustrations, the radii (in red) make same angle with shell outline at all points

The equiangular spiral is very common in nature. Apart from the nautilus shell, such curves, or short sections of them, can be seen in the arms of spiral galaxies, the horns and tusks of animals, and the claws of birds.

The spiral can be found in vegetation, too. For example, the florets in the centre of a daisy, the scales on a pine cone, and even the sticks in a bunch of celery all show spiral growth.

A Mathematical Tombstone

Jacob Bernoulli, a member of a famous and influential Swiss family of mathematicians, asked that a spiral curve be inscribed on his grave stone.

Jacobus Bernoulli
1654-1705
Resurgam

JACOBUS
BERNOULLI
1654 - 1705
·Resurgam·

23

CHAPTER 3 – BANDS, MAPS AND NETWORKS

BANDS

The Möbius Band

Augustus Möbius (1790 – 1868) was a German mathematician and astronomer who was one of the founders of a branch of mathematics called **topology**. Topology is a topic in which shapes and spaces do some rather unlikely things.

The Möbius Band is a good example of topology, as the following experiment will show:

1 Cut a strip of paper at least 30cm long and about 3cm wide:

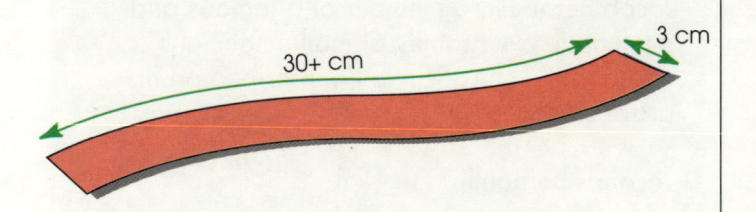

2 Put a piece of sticky tape on one end and hold the ends in the shape of an ordinary loop. But then give one end half a twist (through 180 degrees) before the ends are joined:

This produces a Möbius Band, which has some curious properties.

1 Try writing one word round the outside of the band, and a different word round the inside:

Look at what happens (see answers, pages 46–47).

24

BANDS, MAPS AND NETWORKS

2 Now take a pair of scissors and cut down the centre line of the band:

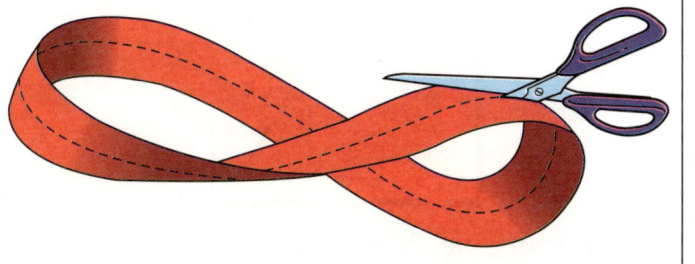

Again, look at what happens. (See answers, pages 46-47.)

3 Make a second Möbius Band, but this time cut round a third of the way from its edge.

4 Continue until the cut has taken two trips round the band before coming back to where it started:

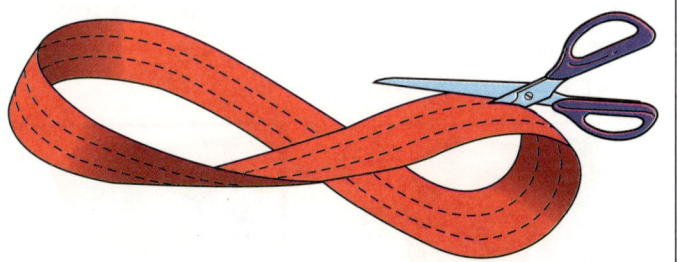

What is the result? (See answers, pages 46-47.)

If you've done the experiments above, you'll understand this poem:

> *A mathematician confided*
> *That a Möbius Band is one-sided*
> *And you'll get quite a laugh*
> *If you cut one in half*
> *For it stays in one piece*
> *when divided*

25

MAPS

The Map Problem

Augustus Möbius is also thought to have been responsible for a famous and long-standing problem to do with colouring maps. In 1840 he is said to have given his students a question along these lines.

We <u>could</u> use three colours to shade this map, so that neighbouring countries are coloured differently:

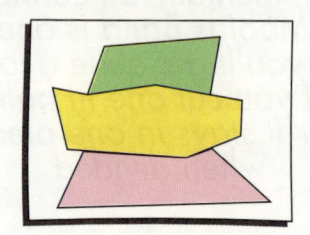

But we could do it with only two colours:

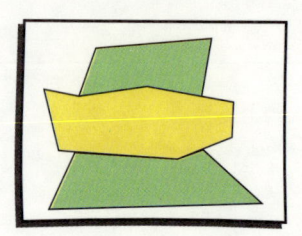

This map, however, really <u>does</u> need three colours:

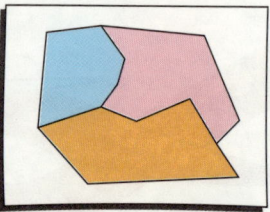

And this one needs four colours:

But – Möbius suggested to his students – you can never have a map that needs more than four colours. Of course, it is possible to invent maps that use more than four colours, but they never really need them.

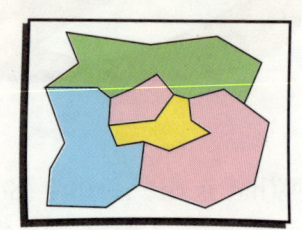

BANDS, MAPS AND NETWORKS

Copy these 'maps' and see how few colours it is possible to use, making sure that neighbouring 'countries' are coloured differently.

Find an atlas and look at the way countries or regions have been coloured. Try tracing a map and see if it is possible to use fewer colours than the printers.

Professor Möbius' students discussed the problem and tried out very many maps before deciding that that no map needed more than four colours. Möbius then asked them to come up with a mathematical proof to show that more than four is unnecessary. Sadly, they couldn't do it, and neither could the Professor, and the 'four-colour problem' became a famous mathematical puzzle that many mathematicians tackled but failed to solve. That is, until 1976, when an American mathematician used a computer to produce an answer – 136 years after Möbius had set the question. The complex computer result proved that the no-more-than-4-colours conjecture was true.

(See answers, pages 46-47.)

27

NETWORKS

The Bridges of Königsberg

The Prussian city of Königsberg was the source of the famous Königsberg bridge problem 200 years ago.

Königsberg was divided by the River Pregel, and seven bridges joined together the various parts of the city.

The citizens of Königsberg had believed for some time that it might be possible to go for a walk and cross over all the bridges without going over any bridge more than once. Use the illustration to try the problem and see if you can cross all of the bridges, but no bridge more than once. Start and finish where you like.

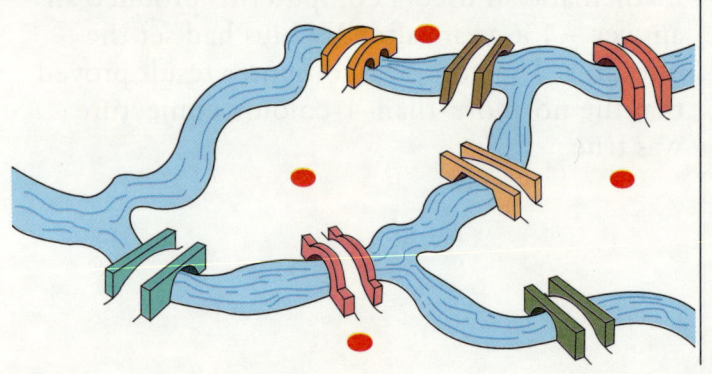

A Swiss mathematician, Leonhard Euler (1707 – 1783), heard of the Königsberg bridges and set out to discover what he could about the problem.

First, he made a topological map of Königsberg, turning the land masses into dots and the bridges into lines – a mathematical network, in fact.

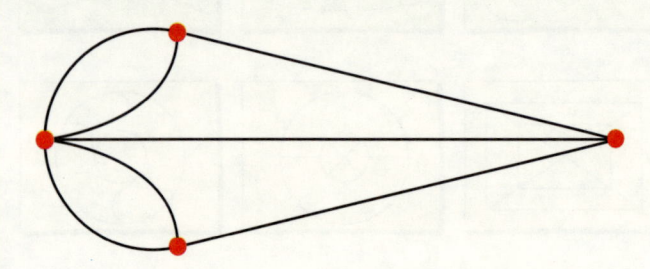

Then he looked at the dots and noticed that there was an odd number of lines joined to each, and after investigating a number of topological maps that he'd devised himself, he came up with a rule along these lines:

It is possible to trace out a network as long as there are not more than 3 points with an odd number of lines meeting at them.

BANDS, MAPS AND NETWORKS

For example, look at the network below. It's quite well known and you may have seen it before. What people often ask is "Can you draw this without taking your pencil off the paper or going over any line twice?"

There are only two odd points, which is less than Euler's limit of three, so it should be possible to draw it.

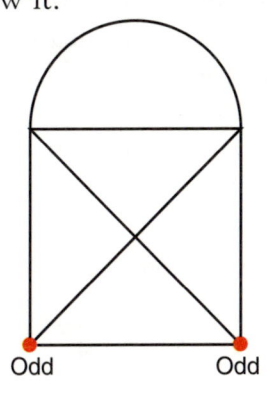

Try it out.

A final word before you begin. Mathematically, if we can draw a network without taking off our pencil or repeating a line, we say we can traverse it.

Look at the networks below, and then use Euler's rule to decide which of them can be traversed. Try drawing the networks that you decided it's possible to traverse. (See answers, pages 46-47.)

THE 'ENVELOPE' NETWORK
Were you right?

Now try to invent some traversable networks and try them out on a friend.

29

BANDS, MAPS AND NETWORKS

More about Topological Maps

On an Ordnance Survey map, a midlands railway line looks like this:

But on a train timetable it appears like this:

That's because people who travel on the train don't really need to know the distances between stations or how the line curves. All they need to know is the relative positions of the stations. So they get a topological map, in which real features are turned into a diagram, in much the same way as Euler turned Königsberg into a network. If you can get a copy of a local route map, compare it with the real shape of the route on an Ordnance Survey or town plan map.

One of the most famous of topological maps appeared in 1931. It was a map of the London Underground rail system and it was prompted by the need to make a simplified version of what had become a very complicated network of routes. The designer was Harry Beck, and although extra lines have been added to the map over the years as new routes have been constructed, his original idea is still used. If you can find a street map of London that shows Underground stations, try comparing it with Harry's map and see what a complicated problem he solved.

The London Underground

Registered user number. 96/2435

MORE ABOUT NETWORKS

A Formula for Networks

Earlier in this chapter, the terms 'points' and 'lines' were used. However, the correct mathematical vocabulary should be 'nodes' instead of points and 'arcs' instead of lines. There is also the idea of a region.

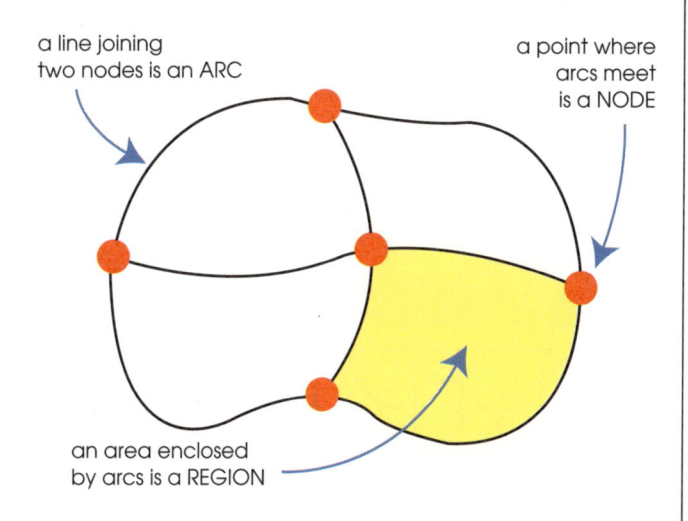

a line joining two nodes is an ARC

a point where arcs meet is a NODE

an area enclosed by arcs is a REGION

In the network above there are:
- 5 nodes
- 4 regions
- 8 arcs

By itself, that's not a particularly remarkable result, but if you carry out an experiment in which you count the numbers of nodes, regions and arcs in a number of networks, then you should start to see a special connection between the numbers.

1 Start by making a table of results (always good practice in mathematics). Copy the table below. The numbers for the network above are already in place:

NETWORK	NODES	REGIONS	ARCS
1	5	4	8
2			
3			
4			
5			
6			

BANDS, MAPS AND NETWORKS

2 Now count and enter the numbers of nodes, regions and arcs for more networks. Use the networks on page 29 that you were testing for traversability, or you can invent some of your own.

3 When the table has been filled in, look at the results and see if there is a connection between the numbers of nodes, regions and arcs.

Try writing the connection as a mathematical **formula**. That is, instead of words use 'N', 'R' and 'A' in combination with whatever mathematical symbols you might need, like +, -, x, ÷ and =. (See answers, pages 46-47.)

Equivalent Networks

Topology is sometimes called 'rubbersheet geometry', because it deals with the way shapes can be distorted but remain topologically equal. An example of this distortion was used earlier, when geographical maps became topological maps.

Here's an example of a rubbersheet distortion of an original network:

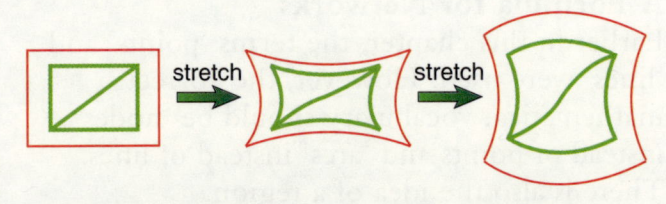

Topologically speaking, the networks are equivalent, because although arcs have been stretched and curved, nodes have changed position and regions have changed shape, nothing has been broken or newly joined.

Here are more examples of topological equivalents:

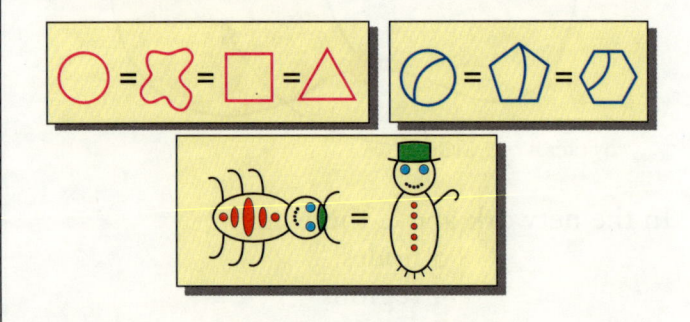

BANDS, MAPS AND NETWORKS

Here are 12 networks, made up of six topologically equivalent pairs. Try to find the pairs. (See answers, pages 46-47.)

33

CHAPTER 4 – CUTTING UP A CONE

Conic Sections

In chapter 1, we looked at the mathematical meaning of dissection. To introduce this chapter, you need to do a three-dimensional dissection, for which you'll need a lump of clay or Plasticene and a length of thin wire – something like cheese-cutting wire.

1 Roll the clay into a cone shape. This isn't easy, so be patient. Try using a rolling board to help get straight edges:

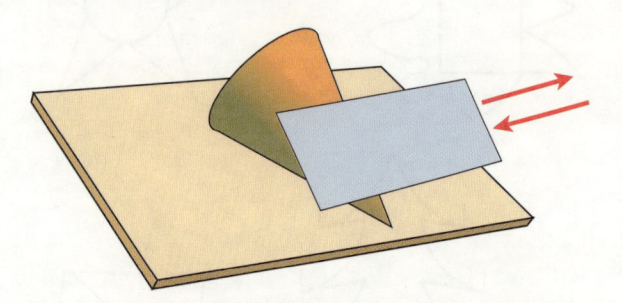

2 When you're satisfied with the cone, make two cuts through it with the wire, one cutting off the top at an angle and one parallel to an edge:

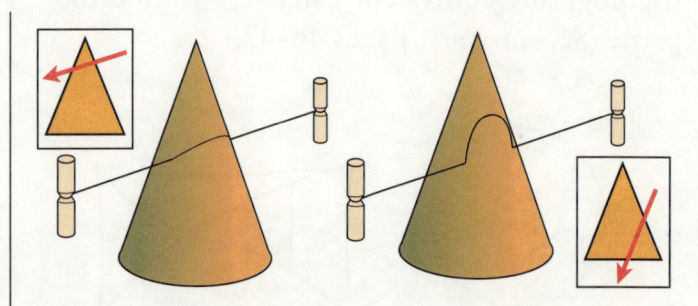

Look at the cut faces. There should be two curves. These curves are part of a family of curves known as the **conic sections**.

The Ellipse

It is possible to see ellipses every day. Every time a circle is looked at from an angle, it becomes an ellipse.

CUTTING UP A CONE

An ellipse can be made by folding, using an envelope method similar to those used in chapter 1:

1 Draw a circle on paper with a radius of around 8cm.

2 Then cut out the circle very carefully and mark a point 'F' about 4cm from its circumference. (Note that 'around' and 'about' don't sound very precise, but exact dimensions aren't critical in this envelope, and in fact you might try experimenting with different circle radii and positions of F to see how they affect the result.):

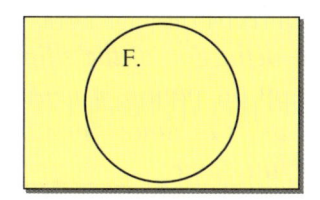

3 Now fold the circle so that the circumference is touching the point F, making the crease very sharp so that it shows clearly on the paper:

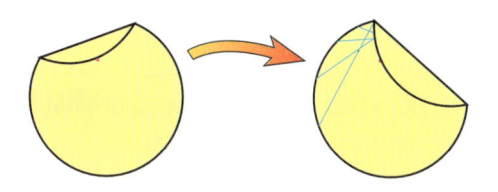

4 Fold the circle many times, taking a new position for the crease each time, folding to F and working right round the circumference:

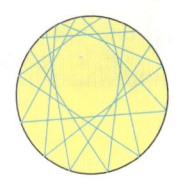

The result should be an ellipse, made from an envelope of straight creases. The shape of the ellipse should be clear, but it can be made clearer by going over the creases with a pencil and ruler.

Alternatively, cut the original circle from good quality tracing paper, as the creases will make white lines in the paper.

35

CUTTING UP A CONE

The reason we called the guide point 'F' in the folding experiment is because it is at one focus of the ellipse. Focus is Latin for 'hearth', and the word was used to describe that point when astronomers discovered that the sun – a mighty 'hearth' – is at one focus of the elliptical orbits in which the planets travel.

Mention of 'one focus' might indicate that an ellipse has more than one, and that is correct. Here's a method for drawing an ellipse that uses the fact that it has two foci:

1 Stick two pins through a piece of paper on a thick card base board.

2 Make a loop of thread to go over the pins, leaving some slack.

3 Now pull the loop taught with a pencil and move the pencil around the paper, keeping the thread taught. You may need to experiment with the size of your loop if you run off the paper, but eventually you'll produce an ellipse with the pins at its foci:

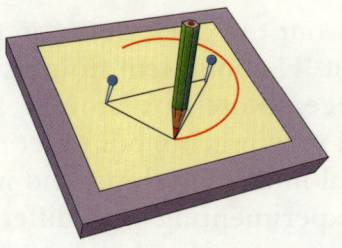

4 When you've seen how the method works, try changing the positions of the pins and the size of the loop.

A mathematical definition of the ellipse is:
A curve formed by the path of a point which moves so that the sum of its distances from two points A and B is always the same.

X + Y is always the same

Can you see how your string-and-pins method follows this definition?

The Parabola

The parabola, like the ellipse, is another 'everyday' curve. Whenever a ball is thrown through the air, its path is a parabola. The reflectors in torches and headlights are parabolic, as are satellite TV dishes, and the curve made when the ends of a chain necklace are held is very close to a parabola.

It's possible to paper-fold a parabola in the same way that an ellipse was folded, that is, using an envelope method:

1 Start with a rectangle of paper and mark a point 'F' in the centre of the paper and about 3cm from one of the short edges:

2 Now fold the short edge so that it goes through F, and make a sharp crease:

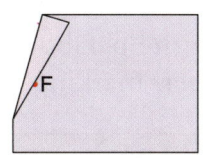

3 Make lots of folds like this, and, as before, highlight them with pencil lines to form a clear parabola:

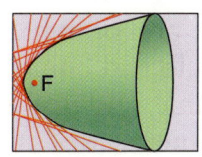

'F' is the focus of the parabola. Imagine the parabola spinning on its axis to make a bowl shape, and then imagine that the bowl is a reflector – F is where the light bulb would be placed relative to the reflector. In a parabolic satellite dish, the signal receiver is also placed at the focus of the curve of the dish.

CUTTING UP A CONE

Try an experiment to demonstrate the reflector/receiver properties of a parabolic dish, using the parabola envelope just drawn:

1 Carefully trace the parabola outline onto a clean sheet of paper, marking the position of the focus:

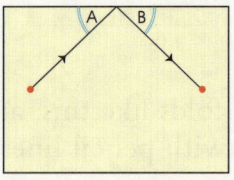

2 Now, imagine that the focus is a light bulb and the parabola is a reflector and try to draw in the lines of the rays of light. The rays will shoot from the bulb and bounce off the reflector in the same way that a snooker ball bounces off a cushion – that is, so that the angles A and B are the same:

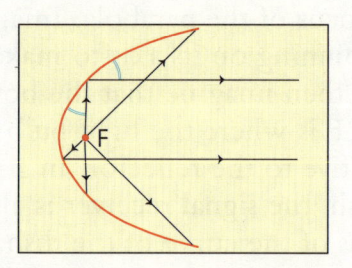

Try lots of 'rays' from the focus bulb, and see where they bounce to after hitting the reflector. Do the reflected rays make a beam parallel to the reflector axis? If so, this shows why reflectors are parabolic. If the same method is used with a reflector based on a circle, the reflected rays will bounce in all directions.

Parabolic receivers – radar dishes and radio telescopes, as well as the TV satellite dishes – use the same principle as reflectors, but in the opposite direction. That is, signals come into the dish and are reflected to the signal receiver.

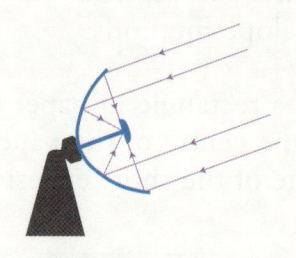

The parabolic curve followed by objects thrown through the air is not always easy to see, although jets of water in a fountain can be good examples.

CUTTING UP A CONE

With a board, a large piece of paper, a marble and some runny paint, it is possible to make a moving-object parabola path:

1 Support the board at one end to make a shallow slope, and clip the paper to it.

2 Stir the marble around in the paint to coat it, and then roll it gently up the slope. With practice, you'll find that a smooth parabolic paint curve results:

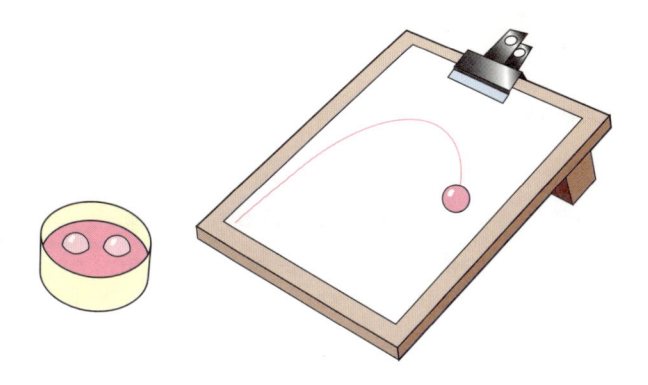

Make sure you put down plenty of newspaper to catch the marble when it rolls off the board, and have a supply of damp paper towels.

A good quality speaker cabinet often has a combination of 'tweeters' for high sounds and 'woofers' for low sounds.

As a compromise, some speakers are elliptical, the narrow part acting as a tweeter and the wide part acting as a woofer.

Comets

Comets are giant chunks of ice and dust particles that travel through space and are sometime visible from earth. Comet Hyakutake was very clear in 1996.

Some comets travel in elliptical paths around the solar system, while others come out of, and return to, deep space. In both cases, the sun is at the focus of the comet's path.

Note that the 'tail' of a comet is blown away from the sun by solar radiation.

CHAPTER 5 – SOLID FOUNDATIONS

The Platonic Solids

In parts of the world where the sea water is warm, floating near to the surface can be found minute creatures called **radiolarians**. These creatures are so small they can only be seen under a powerful microscope, but they look like this:

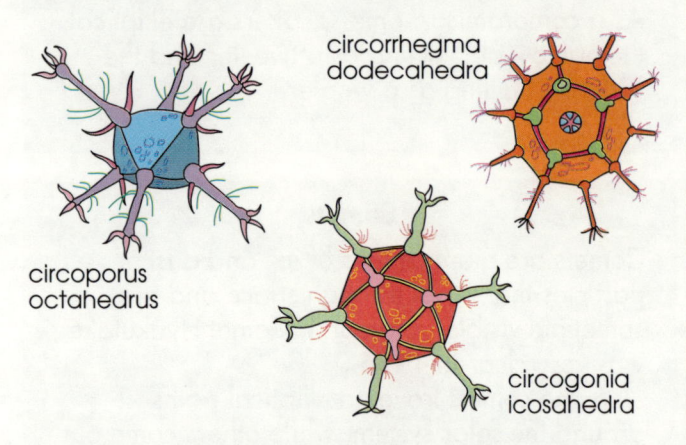

circoporus octahedrus

circorrhegma dodecahedra

circogonia icosahedra

The skeleton surfaces of circoporus and circogonia are made of equilateral triangles, and the surface of circorrhegma is made of regular pentagons. These tiny life forms show the shapes of three of the five **Platonic solids**:

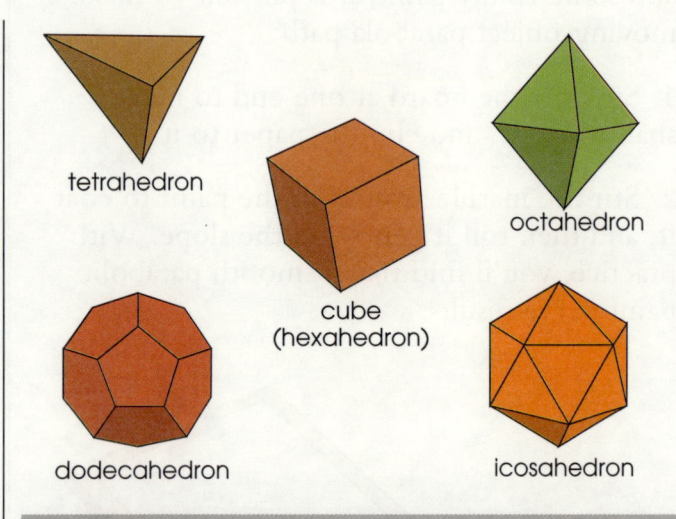

tetrahedron

cube (hexahedron)

octahedron

dodecahedron

icosahedron

Plato's Academy

Plato (428-348BC) was one of the greatest of Greek mathematicians and founded his academy for the study of mathematics and philosophy around 380BC. Over the entrance to the academy was a sign which read 'let no-one enter who is ignorant of geometry'

Μηδεις Λγεωμετρητος Εισιτω

The Platonic solids are also known as 'regular' solids, because a regular solid has identical corners, edges and faces. The ancient Egyptians knew about tetrahedrons, cubes and octahedrons, and Theaetetus, a member of Plato's Academy, proved that only five such solids could exist. Oxford mathematician, Charles Dodgson, better known as Lewis Carroll, author of *Alice in Wonderland*, said that the Platonic solids were "provokingly few in number".

The Greeks believed that all matter was made from different combinations of the four elements: fire, earth, air and water. Plato went further and said that the smallest particles – or atoms – of the elements must be shaped like the regular solids.

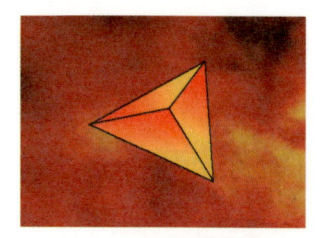

earth atom

water atom

To complete the picture, he suggested that the universe was shaped liked a dodecahedron.

fire atom

air atom

Modelling the Solids
The Platonic solids can be made in various ways. The first method is fairly straightforward and uses conventional nets, which will need to be cut from card.

Use square and equilateral triangle paper as the basis for all but the dodecahedron net. If there is no triangular paper, it can be made by producing lots of joined equilateral triangles by drawing circles with a pair of compasses:

SOLID FOUNDATIONS

1 Draw a circle:

2 Then draw another:

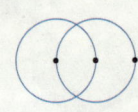

3 And here, etc:

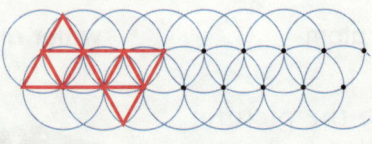

Keep going. The method will become clear and, eventually, a mass of circles will be created onto which the triangular nets can be drawn:

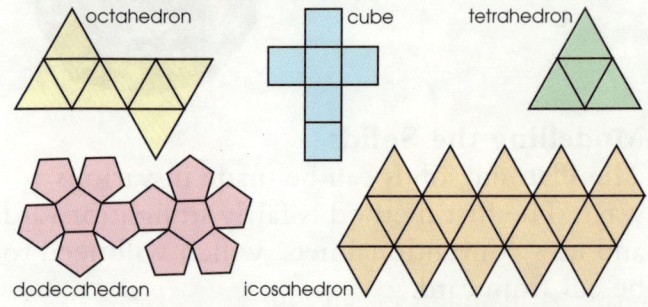

octahedron   cube   tetrahedron

dodecahedron   icosahedron

In the nets shown above, the gluing flaps have been left out to make the net's construction clearer, but they will need to be added. Also make sure flaps are not added where they are not required.

To construct the regular pentagons for the dodecahedron net, use a pair of compasses and a protractor to draw a circle of radius 3cm, and draw in a radius:

1 Measure angles of 72 degrees from the radius.

2 Then draw four more radii:

3 Join the tips of the radii:

This will produce a regular pentagon which can be used as a template to draw the dodecahedron net.

42

SOLID FOUNDATIONS

Provokingly Few in Number

Lewis Carroll was correct. There are surprisingly few regular solids. To discover why this should be so, try making regular solids with faces that are:

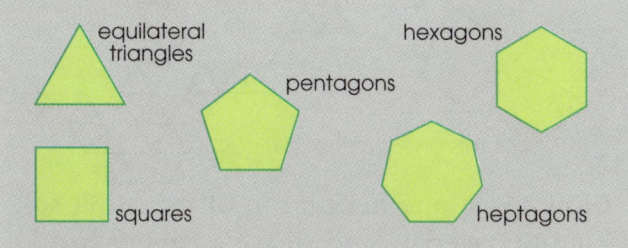

- equilateral triangles
- squares
- pentagons
- hexagons
- heptagons

Did you have any success with the last two? (See answers, pages 46-47.)

Plaited Solids

Plaiting is a more unusual way of making solids. It was first described in the 1888 book *Plaited Crystal Models*, by John Gorham of Tonbridge in Kent.

Plaiting methods need no sticking flaps or glue. The paper nets are simply folded until a single flap remains, which is tucked in to secure the model.

To make a plaited tetrahedron, cut the net below from paper – fairly stiff if possible, but not card. The triangles are, of course, equilateral. Remember the triangle construction method used for the last section.

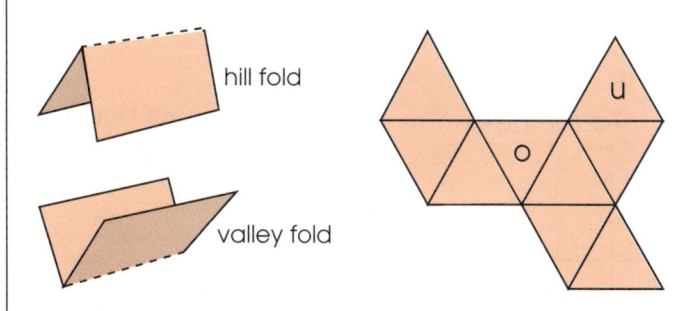

Remember, the triangles must be very accurate.

1 Fold the net into sharp creases on all the lines, so that all folds are hill folds. Be very careful to make the creases exactly on the lines.

2 Now fold the 'O' (over) triangle on top of the 'U' (under) triangle and at once the tetrahedron can be seen starting to form.

SOLID FOUNDATIONS

3 Continue folding and plaiting until the final flap has been tucked in.

The nets shown below are more difficult so make sure the initial construction is very accurate, and fold all lines very carefully into hill folds. In each case, start by folding 'O' onto 'U' and continue until the final flap tucks in:

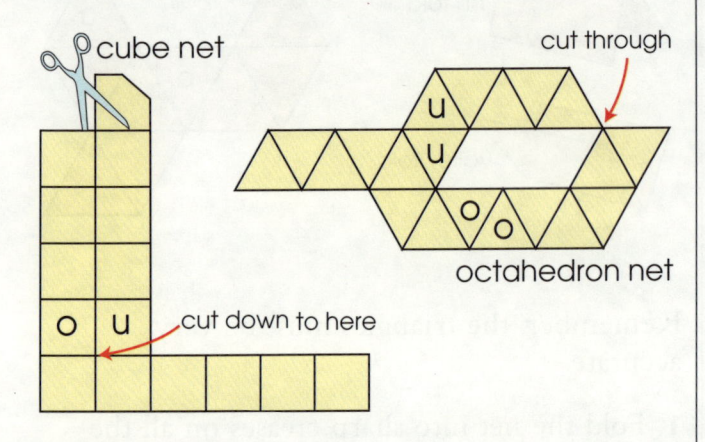

cube net

cut through

octahedron net

cut down to here

A Jumping Dodecahedron
The dodecahedron was left out of the plaiting section. The method that follows isn't a plait, but it does supply an unusual way of making a Platonic solid – it puts itself together:

1 Use the template which was made earlier to draw the two nets shown below onto thick card, scoring on the dotted lines:

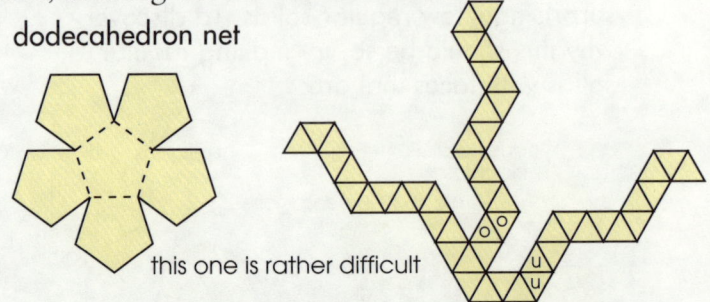

dodecahedron net

this one is rather difficult

2 Now place one net on top of the other so that points overlap, and weave a rubber band over and under the points, like this:

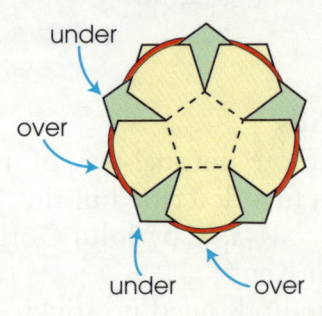

under

over

under over

3 When the rubber band is in place, hold the double net flat on a table and then let it go. The result should surprise you.

SOLID FOUNDATIONS

A Tetrahedron Puzzle
Cut two of these nets from thin card, and make two solids by folding and sticking. The solids will make a tetrahedron when held together in the correct way.

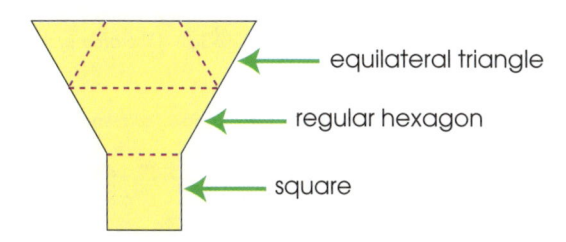

← equilateral triangle
← regular hexagon
← square

Golden rectangles and the Icosahedron
In chapter two, the relationship between the golden rectangle and art and nature was introduced. Golden rectangles have a connection with the Platonic solids, too. To see why, try this experiment:

1 Cut three golden rectangles from thick card. 10cm by 16cm is a convenient size.

2 Cut slots in the rectangles as shown, so that the slots are the same width as the card's thickness:

3 Now fit the three pieces of card together to make a construction that looks like this:

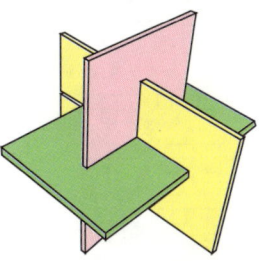

4 The final task is to glue strips of paper between all corners on the construction:

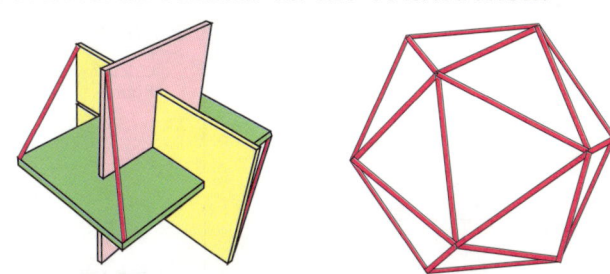

This is the skeleton outline of a regular icosahedron.

45

ANSWERS

Page 10:

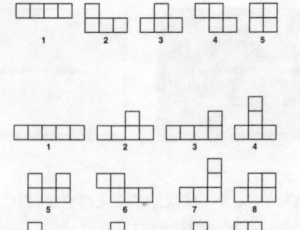

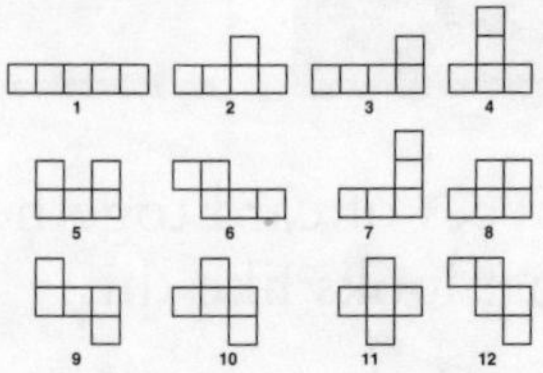

Page 11:

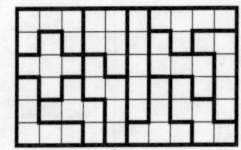

Page 11:

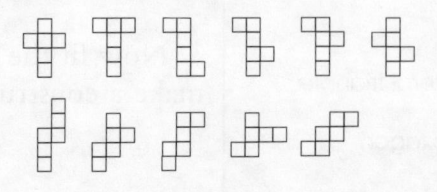

Page 12:

Page 13:
Boat, Shark, Parallelogram, Fox, Rectangle, Triangle, Candle

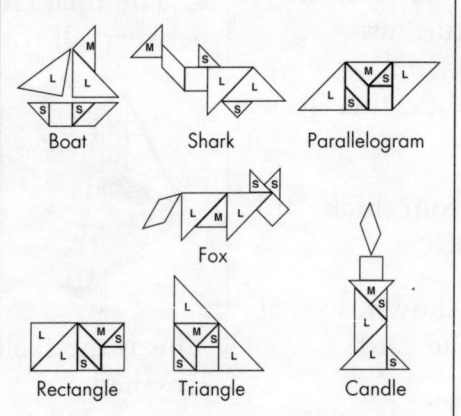

Page 14:

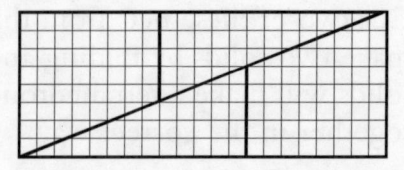

The four pieces rearrange to make this rectangle with an area of 168cm². The area of the square was 169cm².

Page 17: The Fibonacci sequence to 20 places:

1,1,2,3,5,8,13,21,55,89,144,233,377,610, 987,1597,2584,4181,6765

Fibonacci sequence calculations:
a) 1,1,2 ⟶ 1x1=1   1x2=2
   1,2,3 ⟶ 2x2=4   1x3=3
   2,3,5 ⟶ 3x3=9   2x5=10

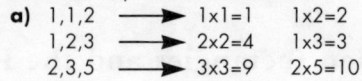

144,233,377 ⟶ 233x233=54289
              144x377=54288

The difference between the solutions is always one, no matter how big the Fibonacci numbers in the sequence of three.

b) 1÷1=1   2÷1=2   3÷2=1.5   5÷3=1.666...
   8÷5=1.6   13÷8=1.625   21÷13=1.615
   34÷21=1.619   55÷34=1.617
   89÷55=1.618   144÷89=1.618
   233÷144=1.618   344÷233=1.618
The answer gets closer and closer to 1.618, and then continues at that value, no matter how many more Fibonacci numbers are taken.

46

ANSWERS

Page 21:
There are two Fibonacci sequences:
27,43,70,113,183 and 86,140,226
and division of a number by the number before it give results close to the golden ratio.

Page 22: The average height ÷ navel height usually comes close the 1.6, the golden ratio.

Page 24–25:

a) A Mobius band has only one side. If you write your name down on one side, you will go all the way round and back to where you started.

b) A Mobius band cut down the middle results in one large band.

c) A Mobius band cut 1/3 of the way from its edge results in two linked bands.

Page 27:

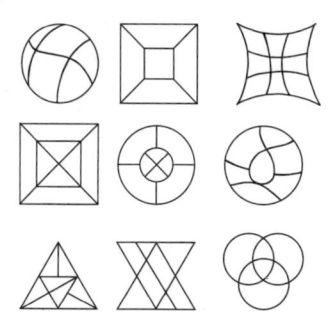

Page 29:

Page 29: Only one of the networks won't traverse.

These will

Page 32: N=R=A+1 and it works for any network.

Page 31:

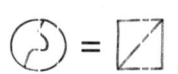

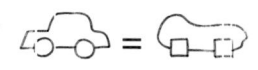

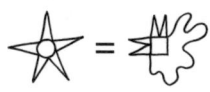

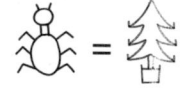

Page 40: It is possible to make regular solids with faces that are equilateral triangles, squares and pentagons because the faces will join together and still leave room for folding up.

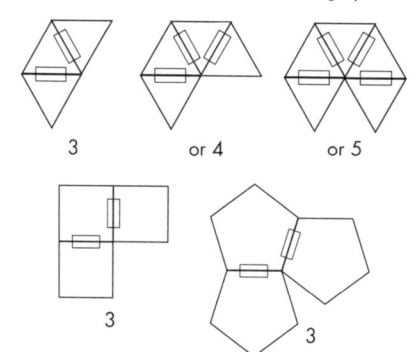

3   or 4   or 5

3   3

However, it is not possible to join 3 hexagons or heptagons (or any regular polygon with more sides) and still leave room for folding.

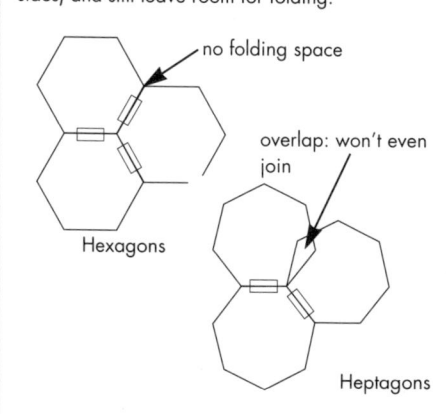

no folding space

overlap: won't even join

Hexagons

Heptagons

47

GLOSSARY

Cardioid: a heart-shaped curve
Conic section: a curve formed by cutting a cone to produce a flat face
Constant width curve heptagon: a seven-sided curve whose distance across from edge-to-edge is always the same, no matter where it is measured, e.g., 20p and 50p pieces
Constant width curve: a curve whose distance across from edge to edge is always the same, no matter where it is measured
Envelope curve: a curve made from a series of straight lines
Fibonacci numbers: a series of numbers each of which is produced by adding the two preceding numbers
Golden rectangle: a rectangle whose length is 1.618 times its width. Its proportions are thought to be visually pleasing
Lissajou figure: a curve produced by combining movements in two different directions
Net: a two-dimensional shape that will fold up to make a three-dimensional solid
Platonic solid: one of the five solids (tetrahedron, cube, octahedron, dodecahedron, icosahedron) described by Theaetetus, a member of Plato's Academy. Each solid is defined as 'regular' because its faces, edges and corners are all the same.
Polyomino: a two-dimensional shape made by joining equal squares edge-to-edge
Radiolarian: a minute sea creature with a skeleton shaped like a Platonic solid
Sector: the area enclosed by two radii of a circle and the part of the circumference between them
Topology: a branch of mathematics that studies the properties of geometrical shapes that stay 'topographically' the same even when distorted
Wankel engine: an engine that uses a constant width curve rotor rather than conventional pistons
Watts drill: a drill, with a cross-section based on a constant width curve, that will produce square holes

INDEX

Atom 41
   fire 41
   air 41
   earth 41
   water 41
Bernoulli, Jacob 23
Cardioid 5
Carroll, Lewis 41, 43
Circogonia icosahedra 40
Circoporus octahedrus 40
Circorrhegma dodecahedra 40
Conic section 34
Constant width curve 6, 7, 9
Constant width curve heptagon 7
Constant width curve triangle 8, 9
Cube 11, 41
Curve, from a straight line 4
   envelope 4, 6
da Vinci, Leonardo 18, 20
Dissection 12, 14, 34
Dodecahedron 41, 42, 44
   jumping 44
Dodgson, Charles 41
Domino 10
Durer, Albrecht 20
Ellipse 34, 35, 36, 37
Envelope curve, see curve
Equilateral triangles 40, 41, 43
Escher, Maurits 15, 16
Euler, Leonhard 28, 29, 30
Fibonacci numbers 17
Golden, section 18
   ratio 10, 18, 20, 21, 22
   rectangle 18, 20, 21, 22, 23, 45
   proportion 21
Golomb, Solomon 10
Gorham, John 43
Heptagon 7
Hexagon 12
Hexomino 10, 11

Icosahedron 45
Jumping dodecahedron, see dodecahedron
Königsberg, bridges 28, 30
Le Corbusier 21
Le Modulor 21
Leonardo of Pisa 17
Lissajou, Jules 3
   figures 3, 4
Maps 26, 27, 28, 30, 32
Möbius, Augustus 24, 27
   band 24, 25, 26
Mondrian, Piet 20
Networks 28, 29, 30, 31, 32, 33
Octahedron 41
Parabola 37, 38, 39
Pendulum, sand 2, 4
Pentomino 10, 11
Plaited solids 43
Plato 41
   Academy 41
Platonic solids 40, 41, 44, 45
Polyomino 10
Radiolarians 40
Rectangle 11, 13, 14, 18, 20, 21, 22, 23, 37, 45
Seurat, Georges 20, 21
Tangrams 12, 13
Tessellation 10, 11, 15, 16
Tetrahedron 41, 43, 45
Tetromino 10
Theaetetus 41
Tiles 15, 16
Topology 24, 32
Tromino 6
Vanishing square 14
Wankel engine 8
Watts drill 8

48